C. Watling

Changes

Reader's Corner

C. Wetling

IMAGINATION
An Odyssey Through Language

Changes

Reader's Corner

Gail Heald-Taylor
General Consultant, Language Arts

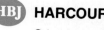 **HARCOURT BRACE JOVANOVICH, PUBLISHERS**

Orlando   San Diego   Chicago   Dallas

Printed in the United States of America

ISBN 0-15-332808-8

Acknowledgments

For permission to reprint copyrighted material, grateful acknowledgment is made to the following sources:

Curtis Brown, Ltd.: "Sunny Days" from *Kim's Place and Other Poems* by Lee Bennett Hopkins. Copyright © 1974 by Lee Bennett Hopkins.
Edith Newlin Chase: "The New Baby Calf" by Edith Newlin Chase from *Very Young Verses.* Copyright 1945, renewed © 1973 by Houghton Mifflin Company.
Delacorte Press/Seymour Lawrence: "Sebastian and the Bee" from *Journeys of Sebastian* by Fernando Krahn. Copyright © 1968 by Fernando Krahn; copyright © 1968 by Dell Publishing Co., Inc.
Dial Books for Young Readers: From *A Boy, a Dog and a Frog* by Mercer Mayer. Copyright © 1967 by Mercer Mayer.
Grosset & Dunlap, Inc.: "The Horses" and the first and second verses from "Or Hounds to Follow on a Track" (Retitled: "I Wonder Where the Clouds Go?") in *The Sparrow Bush* by Elizabeth Coatsworth. Copyright © 1966 by Grosset & Dunlap, Inc.
Harper & Row, Publishers, Inc.: "Okay Everybody" from *Near the Window Tree: Poems and Notes* by Karla Kuskin. Copyright © 1975 by Karla Kuskin. *Harry the Dirty Dog* by Gene Zion, pictures by Margaret Bloy Graham. Text copyright © 1956 by Eugene Zion; pictures copyright © 1956 by Margaret Bloy Graham. "I Wonder" from *All That Sunlight* by Charlotte Zolotow. Copyright © 1967 by Charlotte Zolotow.
Houghton Mifflin Company: From "I Met a Man with Three Eyes" and from "I Met a Man on my Way to Town" in *I Met a Man* by John Ciardi. Copyright © 1961 by John Ciardi.
James Houston: "In summer the rains come" from *Songs of the Dream People,* edited by James Houston. Copyright © 1972 by James Houston.

Macmillan Publishing Company: "The Little Turtle" from *Collected Poems* by Vachel Lindsay. Copyright 1920 by Macmillan Publishing Company, renewed 1948 by Elizabeth C. Lindsay.
Philomel Books: From *The Secret Hiding Place* by Rainey Bennett. Copyright © 1960 by Rainey Bennett. *Daddy, play with me!* by Shigeo Watanabe, pictures by Yasuo Ohtomo. Text copyright © 1984 by Shigeo Watanabe; illustrations copyright © 1984 by Yasuo Ohtomo.
G. P. Putnam's Sons: "After Supper" from *Here, There and Everywhere* by Dorothy Aldis. Copyright 1927, 1928, copyright renewed 1955, 1956 by Dorothy Aldis.
Random House, Inc.: From *He Bear She Bear* by Stan and Jan Berenstain. Copyright © 1974 by Stan and Jan Berenstain.
Marian Reiner, on behalf of Eve Merriam: "Toaster Time" from *There Is No Rhyme for Silver* by Eve Merriam. Copyright © 1962 by Eve Merriam. All rights reserved.
Smithsonian Institution Press: "Send Us a Rainbow" from "Nootka and Quileute Music" by Frances Densmore in *Bureau of American Ethnology Bulletin 124,* p. 285. Published by United States Printing Office, Washington, DC, 1939.
Viking Penguin Inc.: From *Gilberto and the Wind* by Marie Hall Ets. Copyright © 1963 by Marie Hall Ets. *Umbrella* by Taro Yashima. Copyright © 1958 by Taro Yashima; renewed © 1986 by Taro Yashima.
Franklin Watts, Inc.: Adapted from *Heather's Feathers* by Leati Weiss. Copyright © 1976 by Leati Weiss and Ellen Weiss.
Western Publishing Company, Inc.: Adapted from "The Gingerbread Boy" (Retitled: "The Gingerbread Man") in *The Tall Book of Nursery Tales.* © 1944 by Western Publishing Company, Inc.

Art Acknowledgments

Lori Anderson: 41; Peter Aspery: 151; Meg Kelleher Aubrey: 310-313; Willi Baum: 186-205, 220-228; Wendy Biggins: 71; Tom Bobroski: 245; Lisa Bonforte: 236-240; Chuck Bowden: 168, 270, 386 (adapted from photographs from the following sources: 168, John Wheelock Freeman, courtesy Viking Penguin, Inc.; 270, courtesy Delacorte Press/Seymour Lawrence; 386, courtesy Viking Penguin, Inc.); James Buckley: 124, 219; Suzanne K. Clee: 125; Roberta Collier: 321; Kinuko Craft: 52-69; Susan David: 341; Susan Dodge: 249; Tom Dunnington: 342-348; Ted Enik: 3, 27, 185, 206, 309; George Ford: 216; Larry Frederick: 82-88, 388 - 391; Keith Freeman: 153; Kathleen Garry-McCord: 183; Marie-Louise Gay: 122, 123, 130, 131; Margaret Bloy Graham: 278-306; Lane Gregory: 29-32; Marika Hahn: 241, Sharon Harker: 76, 77; Celeste Henriquez: 89; Ann Iosa: 79, 363; Tony Kenyon: 352-356; Christa Kieffer: 132, 133, 172, 173, 246, 247; John Killgrew: 35, 40; Fernando Krahn: 252-269; Judith Lombardi: 175, 357; Laurie Marks: 217, 315; Mercer Mayer: 112-118; Larry Mikec: 44-47, 154-157, 212-215, 317; Mike Muir: 161-167, 169; Tom Noonan: 179, 211; Yasuo Ohtomo: 4-26; Sharron O'Neil: 51; Sue Parnell: 396 (B); Rodney Pate: 329; Steven Petruccio: 137, 150, 158, 171; Debbie Pinkney: 33, 174, 314; Raphael & Bolognese: 36, 37, 326, 327; Roberta Remy: 70, 325, 351; Charles Robinson: 180, 181; Kazuhiko Sano: 318, 319; Gene Sharp: 38, 39; Dan Siculan: 138-149, 248, 320, 390-399; Samantha Carol Smith: 48, 49, 81; Dick Smolinski: 207; Kirsten Soderlind: 331-339; Susan Spellman: 135; Ed Taber: 92-108, 208, 209, 230-233, 272-275, 358-361; Thomas Vroman Associates: 78, 91, 109, 111, 119, 121, 129, 251, 277, 307; Jack Wallen: 387; Jane Yamada: 134; Taro Yashima: 364-385.

Cover: Tom Vroman

Unit Openers: Jane Teiko Oka

Production and Layout: Thomas Vroman Associates

Photo Acknowledgments

Brett Froomer/The Image Bank: 2; Michael Heron/Woodfin Camp: 28; R. Michael Stuckey/Comstock: 34; H. Armstrong Roberts: 42; K. Strand/H. Armstrong Roberts: 50; Taurus Photos: 74; J. Myers/H. Armstrong Roberts: 80; P. Degginger/H. Armstrong Roberts: 90; Stock Imagery: 110; Michael Heron/Woodfin Camp: 120; Picture Cube: 128; David Lissy/Nawrocki Stock Photo: 136; Flip Chalfant/The Image Bank: 152; Alan Pitcairn from Grant Heilman: 159; Galen Rowell/Peter Arnold Inc.: 170; Photo Media/H. Armstrong Roberts: 178; Alan Carey/Photo Researchers, Inc.: 184; Russ Kinne/Comstock: 210; Photri Inc.: 218; Alec Duncan/Taurus Photos: 234; Alan Pitcairn from Grant Heilman: 244; Stephen Dalton/Photo Researchers, Inc.: 250; John T. Turner/FPG: 276; R. Embry/FPG: 308; E.P.I. Nancy Adams/Tom Stack & Associates: 316; David Lissy/Nawrocki Stock Photo: 324; H. Armstrong Roberts: 330; A. Foley/H. Armstrong Roberts: 340; Daemmrich/Click Chicago: 350; Gabe Palmer/Mug Shots/The Stock Market: 362.

v

Contents

1 Let's Go Together   1

Daddy, play with me! A story by Shigeo Watanabe   4
    Think and Read 2 • Think and Discuss 27

Get Ready, Get Set, Go! A picture story   30
    Think and Read 28 • Think and Discuss 32

Sunny Days A poem by Lee Bennett Hopkins   36

I Wonder A poem by Charlotte Zolotow   38
    Think and Read 34 • Think and Discuss 40

CONNECTIONS: A Place to Live (Science)   44
    Think and Read 42 • Think and Discuss 48

The Secret Hiding Place A story by Rainey Bennett   52
    Think and Read 50 • Think and Discuss 70

2 What a Surprise!   73

I Met a Man From two riddles in verse by John Ciardi   76
Think and Read 74 • Think and Discuss 78

CONNECTIONS: Teeth, Teeth, Teeth (Health)   82
Think and Read 80 • Think and Discuss 88

Heather's Feathers A story by Leati Weiss   92
Think and Read 90 • Think and Discuss 109

A Boy, A Dog, and A Frog A story in pictures
by Mercer Mayer   112
Think and Read 110 • Think and Discuss 119

Toaster Time A poem by Eve Merriam   122
Think and Read 120 • Think and Discuss 124

3 I Wonder   **127**

I Wonder Where the Clouds Go? From a poem
by Elizabeth Coatsworth   **130**

Who Has Seen the Wind? A poem by Christina Rossetti   **132**
     Think and Read 128 • Think and Discuss 134

The Little Red Hen and the Grain of Wheat A play
based on an English folk tale retold by Veronica S. Hutchinson   **138**
     Think and Read 136 • Think and Discuss 150

CONNECTIONS: The Seasons (Social Studies)   **154**
     Think and Read 152 • Think and Discuss 158

Gilberto and the Wind From a story by Marie Hall Ets   **161**
     Think and Read 159 • Think and Discuss 169

About MARIE HALL ETS   **168**

Rainbow Days Two American Indian poems   **172**
     Think and Read 170 • Think and Discuss 174

4 Tell Me a Story 177

After Supper A poem by Dorothy Aldis 180
Think and Read 178 • Think and Discuss 182

The Gingerbread Man A play based on an American folk tale 186
Think and Read 184 • Think and Discuss 206

LEARN ABOUT STORIES: **Story Mix-up** 208

The Little Turtle A poem by Vachel Lindsay 212
Think and Read 210 • Think and Discuss 216

The Three Billy Goats Gruff A Norwegian folk tale
collected by P. C. Asbjörnsen and Jörgen E. Moe 220
Think and Read 218 • Think and Discuss 229

LEARN ABOUT STORIES: **One, Two, Three—Surprise!** 230

CONNECTIONS: What Animals Need (Science) 236
Think and Read 234 • Think and Discuss 240

5 Far, Far Away   **243**

Where Go the Boats? A poem by Robert Louis Stevenson   **246**
    Think and Read 244 • Think and Discuss 248

Sebastian and the Bee A story in pictures by Fernando Krahn   **252**
    Think and Read 250 • Think and Discuss 271

About FERNANDO KRAHN   **270**

LEARN ABOUT THE LIBRARY: **Rabbit Gets a Library Book**   **272**

Harry the Dirty Dog A story by Gene Zion   **278**
    Think and Read 276 • Think and Discuss 307

CONNECTIONS: Pets and People (Science)   **310**
    Think and Read 308 • Think and Discuss 314

The Horses A poem by Elizabeth Coatsworth   **318**
    Think and Read 316 • Think and Discuss 320

6 I'm Growing   323

Okay Everybody! A poem by Karla Kuskin   **326**
   Think and Read 324 • Think and Discuss 328

The New Baby Calf A poem by Edith H. Newlin   **332**
   Think and Read 330 • Think and Discuss 339

CONNECTIONS: Penguins (Science)   **342**
   Think and Read 340 • Think and Discuss 349

He Bear, She Bear From the story in verse
  by Stan and Jan Berenstain   **352**
   Think and Read 350 • Think and Discuss 357

LEARN ABOUT STORIES: Story Sounds   **358**

Umbrella From the story by Taro Yashima   **364**
   Think and Read 362 • Think and Discuss 387

About TARO YASHIMA   **386**

WORD SPOT: Words, Pictures, Meanings   **389**

1 Let's Go Together

Think and Read

► Talk. How do you play with your family?

► Listen to the story. Think.
What do Bear and Daddy
pretend to be?

How would you fill in the
drawing?

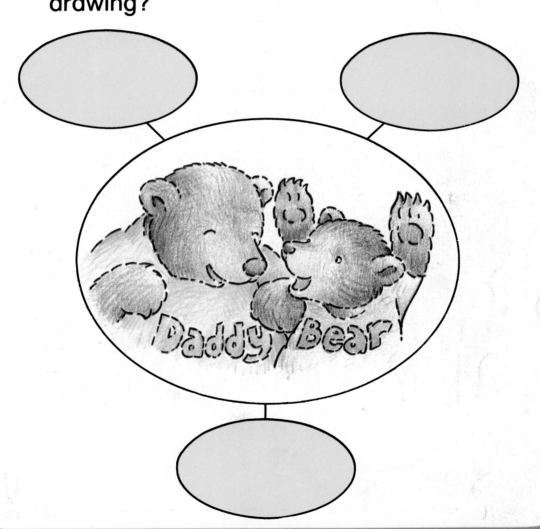

Daddy, play with me!

A story by Shigeo Watanabe
Pictures by Yasuo Ohtomo

I stand on Daddy's feet.
Look! We're dancing!
Right, left. Huff, puff!

Whee! Look how high I am!

Here I go, up on Daddy's shoulders!

Now, Daddy gives me a
piggyback ride.

Daddy's a horse!
Giddyap, giddyap!
Faster, Daddy, faster!

Plop! My horse fell down.
Is he tired?

16

Now, I'm an airplane!
Zoom! Up I go!

I flip over in the air. . .

and kerplunk! I make a safe
landing!

Next, we make a train.

Chug! Chug!

It's hard work.

It's time for a story.
One more, please, Daddy!

Now it's nap time.
Z-z-z-z-z

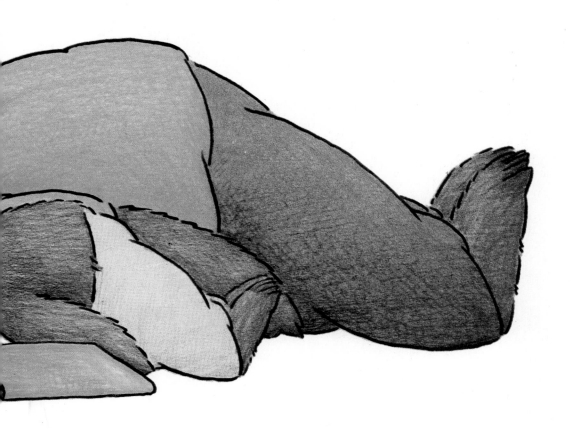

I love to play with Daddy.

Think about the story.
Answer the questions.

1. Who does want to play with? Why?

2. Does have a good time? How do you know?

3. Why do fall asleep?

4. What if played by himself? How would the story be different?

Talk. When is it fun to play with someone? Why?
When do you like to play by yourself? Why?

**WORK WITH
A PARTNER**

Focusing on
"Get Ready, Get Set, Go!"

Think and Read

▶ Talk. What do you do to get ready for school?

► Look at the picture story. Think.
What is each person in the
family doing?

What is each pet doing?

How would you fill in the drawing?

What
are they
doing?

Get Ready, Get Set, Go!

Think about the picture story.
Answer the questions.

1. Where do you think  are going?

2. Why is looking at

the ?

3. How does help?

4. What are the  doing? Why?

5. If you were the artist, what would you add to the picture story?

Talk. How do you help your family?
How does your family help you?

WORK WITH A PARTNER

Focusing on "Sunny Days" and "I Wonder"

Think and Read

▶ Talk. What makes summer special where you live?

► Look at the pictures. Listen to the poems. Think.

What do you see in the city?

What do you see in the country?

What do you see in both places?

How would you fill in the chart?

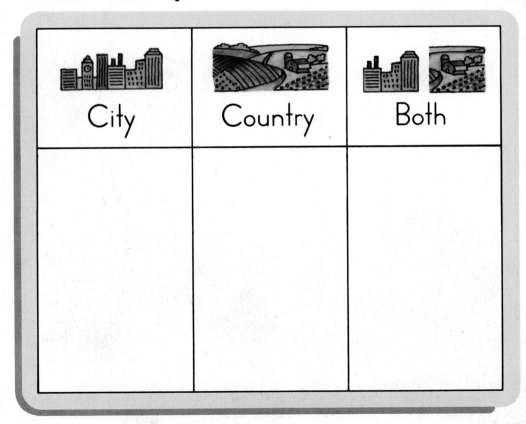

City	Country	Both

Sunny Days

A poem by Lee Bennett Hopkins

Mile-long skyscrapers are my trees.
The subway's *whoosh,* my summer-breeze.

The hydrant is my swimming pool
Where all my friends keep real cool.

The city is the place to be.
The city is the place for me.

Picture by Raphael & Bolognese

I Wonder

A poem by Charlotte Zolotow

A boat steams slowly down the river
this shiny sunny day.
I wonder who is on it
and if it's going far away.

I send good wishes to you,
someone just like me,
wondering who I am on shore
that you can hardly see.

Think about the two poems.
Answer the questions.

1. How are the city and the country different?

2. How are the city and the country alike?

3. Name each picture. Does it belong in the city or the country? Tell why.

a.   b.   c.

4. What other things might city and country children do for fun in the summer?

Talk. How is the place where you live the same as the city?
How is the place different from the city?

Focusing on "A Place to Live"

Think and Read

▶ Talk. Where have you seen wild animals?

► Listen to the information story.
Think about the animals and
the places.

How would you finish this
chart?

Animal	Where the Animal Lives
1.	
2.	

Connections
A Place to Live

This is a river.

Hippos live here.

They eat and drink in the river.

They play in the river, too.

Pictures by Larry Mikec

The river is a home for many
   other animals.
They need the river for food and water.
What animals live here?
What are they doing?

This is a prairie.

Prairie dogs live here.

They dig homes under the ground.

They bark when they are afraid.

The prairie is a home for
many other animals.
They find the food they
need here.
What animals live here?
What are they doing?

Think about the information story.
Answer the questions.

1. Why do the hippos live near a river?

2. Why do the prairie dogs live on the prairie?

3. Which animals live where hippos live? Tell why.

pelican

prairie dog

zebra

4. Which animals live where prairie dogs live? Tell why.

owl

buffalo

fish

Talk. How are the river and the prairie alike?
How are they different?

WORK WITH A PARTNER

Focusing on
"The Secret Hiding Place"

Think and Read

▶ Talk. Why might people want to be alone sometimes?

50

**Listen to the story. Think.
Where do the animals hide?**

**How would you fill in the
drawing?**

Animal	Hiding Place

The
Secret Hiding Place

A story by Rainey Bennett

Pictures by Kinuko Craft

Little Hippo was the pet
of all the hippos.
Every morning the big hippos
waited for him to wake up.
Then they could take care of him.

"Sh," they whispered.
"Little Hippo is sleeping."

"Quiet all!" said Big Charles.

52

And every morning the big hippos
pushed and bumped each other.
    They all wanted to be the first
to bring Little Hippo his breakfast.
    Then they all settled down
to watch Little Hippo eat.

One morning Little Hippo felt cross.

"I don't want my breakfast,"
he said.

"I wish the hippos wouldn't watch
everything I do.

I wish I could be by myself
once in a while."

Big Charles put a cool leaf
on Little Hippo's head.

The leaf shaded him from the sun.

"Don't eat so fast,"
Big Charles said.

Big Charles took Little Hippo
for his morning walk.
All the hippos went along.
"We will protect you,"
said Big Charles.

But Little Hippo didn't want
to be protected.

He wanted to go walking
by himself.

What fun is a walk with
nineteen hippos?

So without even saying
"Excuse me, please," he dashed
toward a bush.

"Stop, Little Hippo,"
Big Charles shouted.

"Birds nest there."

"Don't go in the tall grass.
Zebras hide there.
Do you want to catch stripes?"

Little Hippo stopped to look
at an ostrich with his head
in the sand.
    "Come away, Little Hippo,"
Big Charles shouted.
    "He thinks he's hiding."

Big Charles finally
caught up with Little Hippo.
He was hot and angry.
"That's a chameleon's house,"
Big Charles puffed.
"Come away right now!
When will you learn not to go
looking into secret places?"
Big Charles asked.

Everyone in the jungle
had a hiding place, it seemed.

Everyone but Little Hippo.

The leopard hid in shadowy places.

The tiger hid in the deep grass.

Birds hid in the trees.

Even the elephant was nearly hidden
by leaves as big as his ears.

"You're lucky," Little Hippo told
the turtle and the snail.

"You carry your hiding places
with you.

What's it like inside?"

"It's dark," said the turtle.

"It's dark," said the snail.

Little Hippo was
still cross at lunch.
     But after his nap
there was a big surprise.
     "We will play hide-and-seek,"
Big Charles said.
     "I will be IT."
He leaned against a tree.
     Then he started to count
to five hundred by fives.

5
10
15
20
25
30
35
40

"Now!" Little Hippo whispered.

"Now I can find a hiding place
of my very own.

I'll hide in the river," he said.

"Little Hippo, Little Hippo,
hide with us."

"Oh, no!" Little Hippo said
to himself.

The lion laughed
when he saw Little Hippo
trying to crawl under a rock.
   "Silly hippo," he said.
   "That's no place to hide.
Follow me.
You can hide in my cave."

   "Are we almost there?"
asked Little Hippo.

   "Here we are," said the lion.
   "Make yourself at home."
Then he went hunting for his dinner.

Little Hippo was all alone.
The dark cave was filled
with noises.

"I'm afraid," said Little Hippo.
"I don't want to be alone
this much."

Little Hippo was very frightened.

He ran out of the cave.

He ran for a long, long time.

Finally he sank to the ground
in a little heap.

"Whoof. I can't run any more,"
he said.

Just then the chameleon
put his head out of his house.

"Hello, Little Hippo," he said.

"What are you doing here?"

"I'm lost," said Little Hippo.

"You're lost?" said the chameleon.

"Follow me!"

He led Little Hippo
to the top of a small hill.
"Now, look, Little Hippo!"

And there right below him
was Big Charles.
He and all the other hippos
were looking for something.

66

"Little Hippo, come out,"
they called, pushing through the grass.
"Come out, come out,
wherever you are!" they shouted,
looking under rocks.
But not one of them thought
of looking up.

Little Hippo laughed and laughed.
"They'll never find me," he said.
"They don't see me
even though I'm right up here!"

"Home free! Home free!"
Little Hippo shouted.

    He ran up to Big Charles.

    All the big hippos were so glad
to see him.

    They shouted and stamped their feet.

    "Where did you hide, Little Hippo?

    We looked everywhere,"
said Big Charles.

But Little Hippo didn't tell him.

He just smiled.

He knew that the big hippos

would always look everywhere but up.

And he never told anyone

about his secret hiding place

where he could be alone.

But not too alone.

Think about the story.
Answer the questions.

1. How does feel in the beginning of the story?

2. What happens when plays hide-and-seek?

3. How do you think feels at the end of the story?

4. What does learn about these places?

   a. tall grass   b. dried leaves   c. tree

5. Do you think Little Hippo finds a good hiding place? Tell why or why not.

Talk. Where would you hide if you were an animal? Tell why.

WORK WITH A PARTNER

2 What a Surprise!

Focusing on "I Met a Man"

Think and Read

▶ Talk. What makes you laugh?

▶ Listen to each riddle. Think.
What are the clues?

How would you fill in the charts?

Clues

Riddle 1

? ?

Riddle 2

I Met a Man

From two riddles in verse by John Ciardi

I met a man on my way to town.

He was spinning up, he was spinning down.

He was twice as red as the nose of a clown.

(Mr. Yoyo.)

I met a man that was very wise.
He had no hands, but he had three eyes,
One green, one yellow, and one red.
He had nothing at all but eyes in his head.

(Mr. Traffic Light.)

Pictures by Sharon Harker

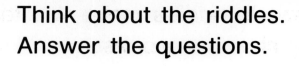

Think about the riddles.
Answer the questions.

1. Which clues help you answer the first riddle?

2. Which clues help you answer the second riddle?

3. What is the answer to each riddle?

4. Why is the title "I Met a Man"?

5. What is funny about each riddle?

Talk. How do riddles make you feel?
Ask your classmate questions.

WORK WITH A PARTNER

Focusing on "Teeth, Teeth, Teeth"

Think and Read

► Talk. How do you use your teeth?

▶ Listen to the information story. Think. How are teeth or beaks used?

How would you fill in the drawing?

Teeth

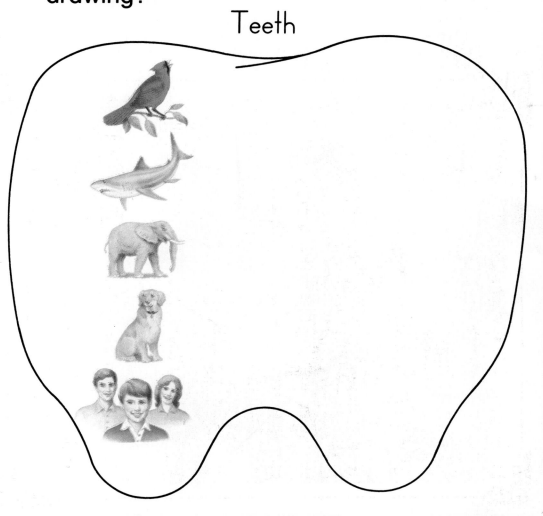

Connections

Teeth, Teeth, Teeth

Birds have beaks, but they do not have teeth.

How do birds use their beaks?

Look at the pictures.

Pictures by Larry Frederick

Sharks have rows of teeth.
Old teeth fall out.
New ones grow in.
How do sharks use their teeth?
Look and see.

Elephants have six teeth.

Four teeth are in the elephant's mouth.

The elephant uses them to chew.

Two teeth are outside.

They are long.

They are strong.

They are called *tusks*.

How does the elephant use its tusks?

Dogs have many teeth.

Dogs rub their teeth clean.

Bones help them clean their teeth.

What else helps them?

Look and see.

People have many small teeth.

What helps them care for
their teeth?

Look and see.

How do you care for your teeth?

The dentist can help take care
of your teeth.

Look at the picture.

How is the dentist helping?

How can you help the dentist?

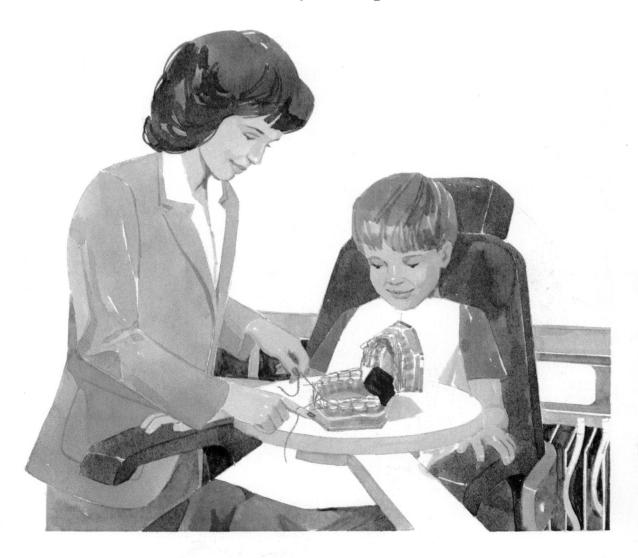

Think about the information story.
Answer the questions.

**Think
and
Discuss**

1. What do birds do with their
   beaks?

2. What do sharks catch with
   their teeth?

3. Why does an elephant have
   tusks?

4. How do dogs clean their
   teeth?

5. Why must people take care of
   their teeth?

Talk. How does your dentist help you?

WORK WITH A PARTNER

Think and Read

▶ Talk. What makes you feel proud?

► Listen to each part of the story.
What happens?
How does Heather feel?

How would you fill in the chart?

HEATHER'S STORY

The Tooth Fairy
What happens?
How does Heather feel?
A Surprise for Heather
What happens?
How does Heather feel?
The Feather Fairy
What happens?
How does Heather feel?

Heather's Feathers

A story by Leatie Weiss

Pictures by Ed Taber

The Tooth Fairy

Heather was the only bird
in her class.

She was the only one with feathers.
She was the only one with a beak.

Everyone thought Heather was great.
She could paint with her wings.
She could win every race.

And then everything changed.

It all began at snack time
one morning.

Robbie was having a hard time
eating his cookie.

"My front tooth is loose," he said.
"I can't wait for it to fall out."
He wiggled it with his paw.

"I lost two teeth already," said Patty.

"I lost four," said Amy.
"How many did you lose, Heather?"

"None," said Heather.
"You can't lose teeth
if you don't have teeth."

"No teeth?" they all asked.

"My beak can do everything
your teeth can do," said Heather.

"It can't get you a present
from the Tooth Fairy," said Robbie.
And they all started laughing
as if they knew a big secret.

Heather felt awful.

Then Robbie began shouting,
"My tooth fell out!"
What a fuss they all made.

"Put it under your pillow tonight,"
said the teacher.
"The Tooth Fairy will leave you
a present."

"So that's what the Tooth Fairy
does," thought Heather.
"What good is a beak?"

The next day Harold had lost
a tooth.

Then Freddy's tooth was loose,
too!

All they did was brag.

"I hate being a bird,"
thought Heather.

"I don't even believe
in the Tooth Fairy.

If she was a real fairy,
she'd help me grow a tooth!"

It was time for Show and Tell.

Heather had brought her toy bear.

But it was Harold's turn first.

He had 50 cents to show

from You Know Who.

"What did you bring today,
Heather?" asked the teacher.

Heather hid her bear.
"I forgot," she said,
and started to cry.

The teacher tried to cheer her up.
Then the bell rang.
It was time to go home.

A Surprise for Heather

It was Father Bird's turn
to drive home that day.
He saw Heather's sad face.

"Cheer up," said Father.
"I have a surprise for you.
I baked a cake
and you can help frost it."

"Who cares about cake?"
cried Heather.
"I want a surprise
from the Tooth Fairy.
I hate being a bird."

"Be proud you're a bird,"
said Father.
"We know a few tricks, too."

"What kind of tricks?"
asked Heather.

"You will see," said Father.
"Maybe someday soon."

"I don't believe it,"
cried Heather.
She gave her feathers a shake.

Feathers popped out!
She flapped her wings.
Out popped some more feathers.
"I'm getting bald!" she shouted.

"You're not getting bald,"
said Father.
"You are molting."

"Molting?" asked Heather.
"What's molting?"

103

"It's your surprise trick.
Your old feathers fall out.
Then bright new ones grow in,"
said Father.

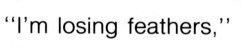

"I'm losing feathers,"
sang Heather.
"That's even better than
losing teeth!"

Heather began to dance.
Her feathers went flying.
She jumped into the pile.
"What do I do with them?"
she asked.

"Put them under your pillow,"
said Father.

"Will the Tooth Fairy come?"
asked Heather.

"No," Father laughed.
"But the Feather Fairy will."

POP

POP

The Feather Fairy

That night, Heather thought
of the feathers under her pillow.
"I'm glad I'm a bird.
Feathers are much softer
to sleep on than teeth!"

The next day Heather got
to school a bit late.

"I have something to show,"
she said.

"I lost lots of feathers
because I am growing up.

And birds have a Feather Fairy!

Wait till you see the presents
she left."

"I wish I had feathers,"
said Robbie.

"You can have some,"
said Heather.

"I got presents for everyone
from the Feather Fairy."

"Aren't we lucky to have Heather
in our class!" said the teacher.

"Oh, yes!" shouted everyone.
"Heather's feathers are better
than the teeth we lost!"

Heather knew it was true.
And she popped out
a few loose feathers to prove it!

Think about the story.
Answer the questions.

surprised   happy   sad

1. What happens first?

2. What happens next?

3. What happens last?

4. How is Heather different from her friends?

5. How is Heather like her friends?

Talk. What lesson did you learn from the story? Ask questions.

WORK IN
A GROUP

Focusing on "A Boy, A Dog, and A Frog"

Think and Read

▶ Talk. When have you been surprised?

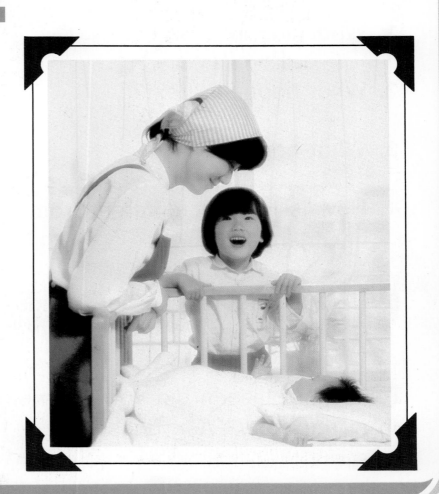

► Read the picture story.
Look at each picture.
Answer these questions.

1. Whom or what do you see?

2. Where are they?

3. What is happening?

A BOY, A DOG, and A FROG

A picture story by Mercer Mayer

3

4

5

6

7

8

9

10

114

11

12

13

14

15

16

17

18

19

20

21

Think about the story.
Answer the questions.

1. How do the and

try to surprise the ?

2. What other things can the

 do to catch the ?

3. Why do the and go home?

4. Why does the follow

the home?

Talk. What might the boy say
to the frog in the tub?

**WORK IN
A GROUP**

**Think
and
Discuss**

119

Focusing on "Toaster Time"

▶ Talk. Tell about helping to make a meal.

▶ Listen to the poem. Think.
Which words rhyme?

How would you fill in the
drawing?

Words That Rhyme

1.
2.
3.
4.

Toaster Time

A poem by Eve Merriam

Tick tick tick tick tick tick tick
Toast up a sandwich quick quick quick
Hamwich
Or jamwich
Lick lick lick!

Tick tick tick tick tick tick—stop!
POP!

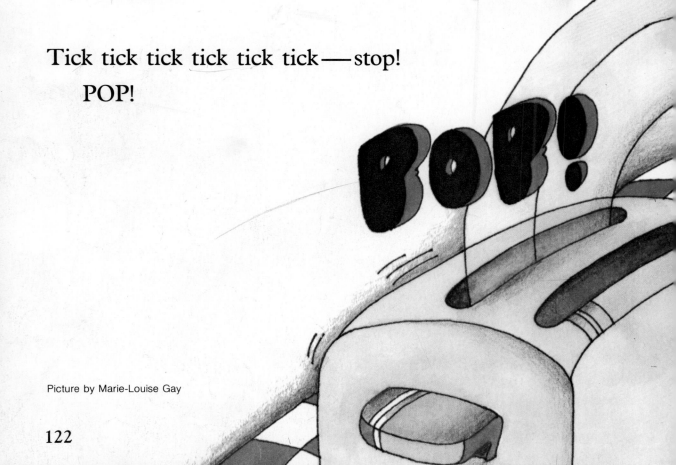

Picture by Marie-Louise Gay

Think about the poem.
Answer the questions.

1. What are the  doing?

2. What words tell how the sounds?

3. What is a <u>hamwich</u>?

4. What is a <u>jamwich</u>?

5. What makes this poem funny?

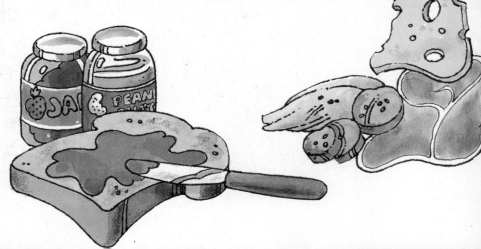

Talk. Tell about another funny
sandwich. Give the funny
sandwich a name.

**WORK WITH
A PARTNER**

3 I Wonder

Think and Read

▶ Talk. What things outside do you wonder about?

128

► Listen to the poems.
Think about the questions the
poets ask.

What would you add to this
drawing?

Questions Poets Ask About Nature
1.
2.
3.
4.
5.

I Wonder Where the Clouds Go?

From a poem by Elizabeth Coatsworth

I wonder where the clouds go?
I wonder what the wind says?
I wonder what it is makes snow?
And how the birds get back?

I wonder how the flowers grow,
So many colors from one earth.
And how it is that feathers know
Which should be brown or red or black?

Pictures by Marie-Louise Gay

131

Who Has Seen the Wind?

A poem by Christina Rossetti

Who has seen the wind?
    Neither I nor you:
But when the leaves hang trembling
    The wind is passing through.

Who has seen the wind?
    Neither you nor I:
But when the trees bow down their heads
    The wind is passing by.

Picture by Christa Kieffer

133

Think about the poems.
Answer the questions.

1. What do the poets wonder about?

2. Which of these things do you wonder about?

3. Where do you think the clouds go?

4. How can you tell when it is windy?

5. What questions would you add to the poems?

Talk about the questions the poets ask.
How can you find the answers?

Focusing on "The Little Red Hen and the Grain of Wheat"

Think and Read

▶ Talk. When have you needed help? What happened?

▶ Listen to the play. Think.
What does Little Red Hen ask
the duck, the cat, and the dog?
How do they answer?

How would you fill in the
chart?

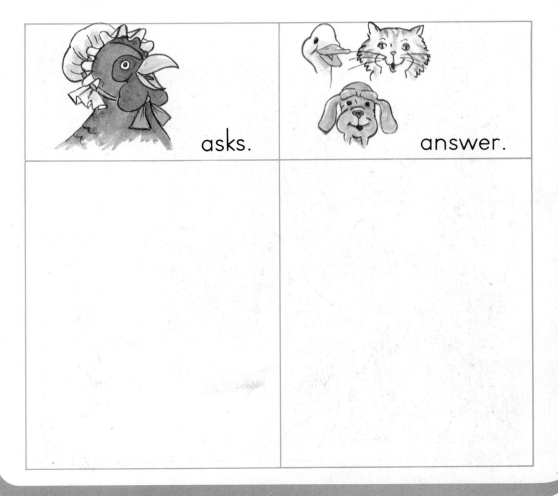

asks.

answer.

The Little Red Hen and the Grain of Wheat

A play based on an English folk tale retold by

Veronica S. Hutchinson

Pictures by Dan Siculan

Characters

Storyteller/Teacher	**Cat**
Little Red Hen	**Dog**
Duck	

Teacher: One day the Little Red Hen was scratching in the farmyard when she found a grain of wheat. "Who will plant the wheat?" she asked. The duck and the cat and the dog answered,

Duck: Not I.

Cat: Not I.

Dog: Not I.

Teacher: But Little Red Hen said,

Hen: Then I will.

Teacher: So the Little Red Hen planted the grain of wheat. And every day she watered the wheat, and pulled the weeds, and watched the wheat grow. After some time, the wheat grew tall and ripe, and it was ready for cutting. "Who will cut the wheat?" asked the Little Red Hen. The duck and the cat and the dog answered,

140

Duck: Not I.

Cat: Not I.

Dog: Not I.

Teacher: But Little Red Hen said,

Hen: Then I will.

141

Teacher: So the Little Red Hen cut and threshed the wheat and when it was threshed, she asked, "Who will take the wheat to the mill to have it ground into flour?" The duck and the cat and the dog answered,

Duck: Not I.

Cat: Not I.

Dog: Not I.

Teacher: But Little Red Hen said,

Hen: Then I will.

Teacher: So the Little Red Hen took the wheat to the mill and brought back a bag of fine, soft flour. "Who will make this flour into bread?" she asked. The duck and the cat and the dog answered,

Duck: Not I.

Cat: Not I.

Dog: Not I.

Teacher: But Little Red Hen said,

Hen: Then I will.

145

Teacher: So the Little Red Hen mixed the flour with honey and milk and butter and yeast and a little pinch of salt. Then she baked a lovely loaf of bread. When the bread was ready she asked, "Now, who will eat the bread?" The duck and the cat and the dog answered,

146

Duck: Oh, I will!

Cat: Oh, I will!

Dog: Oh, I will!

147

Teacher: But Little Red Hen said,

Hen: Oh, no you won't! I will!

148

Teacher: So the Little Red Hen called her chicks and shared the bread with them. They ate the bread to the very last crumb, and the duck and the cat and the dog went hungry.

149

Think about the play.
Answer the questions.

1. What do say

when asks for help?

2. What does do when

no one helps?

3. Look at the pictures. How do

the help?

4. Do you think should

share the bread with ?

Tell why or why not.

Talk about ways you help others in school. Tell how you feel when you help.

WORK WITH
A PARTNER

Think and Read

▶ Talk. What season is it now? Tell about the season.

152

► Listen to the information story.
Think about how the seasons
are different.

How would you fill in the chart?

Fall	Winter	Spring	Summer

Connections

The Seasons

It is fall in my park.

It is getting cool.

Animals are getting ready for winter.

I like to watch the leaves turn red and yellow.

They are coming down.

I like to play in the leaves with my friend.

Pictures by Larry Mikec

It is winter in my park.
The trees have lost their leaves.
Soft snow is falling.
Does it snow where you live?

I put on my warm coat.
I like to play in the snow.

It is getting warm in my park.

It is spring.

Sometimes it rains.

Rain helps the plants grow.

Spring is my favorite season.

I like to look for birds' eggs.

I like to see baby animals
in the trees.

Summer is hot in my park.
Everything is growing.

I put on my shorts.
I like to play under the trees.
It is cooler here.
I play in the park all summer.
Then summer ends and a new
season begins again.

Think about the information story.
Answer the questions.

Think and Discuss

fall   winter   spring   summer

1. How is the tree in the park different each season?

2. What do the animals do each season?

3. Why does the writer like spring best?

WORK IN A GROUP

Talk about your favorite season. Tell why it is your favorite season.

Focusing on "Gilberto and the Wind"

▶ Talk. What things do you and a friend do together?

Think and Read

► Listen to the story. Think.
What do Gilberto and his friend
do?

How would you fill in the
drawing?

Gilberto and His Friend

First	
Next	
Last	

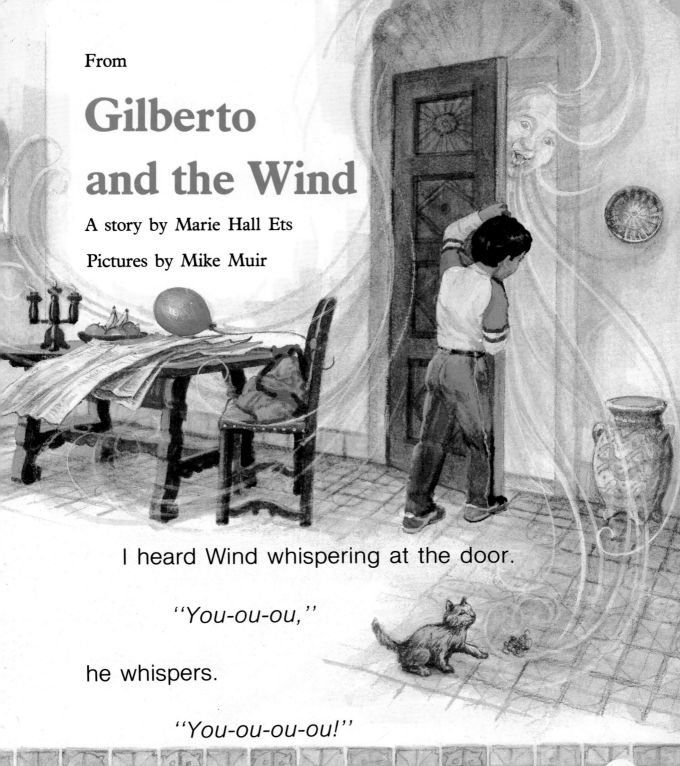

From

Gilberto and the Wind

A story by Marie Hall Ets

Pictures by Mike Muir

I heard Wind whispering at the door.

"You-ou-ou,"

he whispers.

"You-ou-ou-ou!"

So I get my balloon,
and I run out to play.

At first Wind is gentle
and just floats my balloon
around in the air.

But then, with a jerk,
he grabs it away and carries it up
to the top of a tree.

"Wind! Oh, Wind!
Blow it back to me!
Please!"

But he won't.
He just laughs and whispers,

"You-ou-ou-ou!"

163

Wind likes my soap bubbles
best of all.

He can't make the bubbles—
I have to do that.

But he carries them way up
into the air for the sun to color.

Then he blows some back
and makes me laugh when they burst
on the back of my hand.

But then comes a day
when Wind is all tired out.

I whisper,
"Wind, oh, Wind!
Where are you?"

"Sh-sh-sh-sh,"

answers Wind,
and he stirs one dry leaf
to show where he is.

So I lie down beside him
and we both go to sleep—
under the willow tree.

About
MARIE HALL ETS

(To be read by the teacher)

Marie Hall Ets has always felt close to things in nature —animals, trees, flowers, grass, the clouds in the sky. That is why many of her books are about animals and other natural things. Her story Gilberto and the Wind tells of her feelings about the wind and about Gilberto, a boy she met in

California. Now that you have met Gilberto in the story Gilberto and the Wind, you might want to read about him again in the book Bad Boy, Good Boy.

More Books by Marie Hall Ets
Just Me
Another Day
Play with Me
In the Forest
Elephant in a Well

Think about the story.
Answer the questions.

1. What is Gilberto's friend?

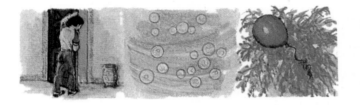

2. How does Wind act like
   Gilberto's friend?

3. Which pictures show when
   Gilberto likes Wind? Tell why.

4. Which picture shows when
   Gilberto does not like Wind?
   Tell why.

5. What else can Gilberto do with
   Wind?

Talk. Tell why you like the wind.
Tell why you do not like the wind.

Think
and
Discuss

**WORK IN
A GROUP**

Focusing on "Rainbow Days"

Think and Read ▶ Talk. Tell about rainbows you have seen.

►Listen to the poems. Think.
What makes a day beautiful?

How would you fill in the
drawing?

What makes
a day beautiful?

1.
2.
3.
4.
5.

Rainbow Days

Two American Indian Poems

In summer the rains come,
The grass grows up,
and the deer has new horns.

—A Yaqui poem

172

You, whose day it is,
Make it beautiful.
Get out your rainbow colors,
So it will be beautiful.

—A Nootka poem

Think about the first poem.
Answer the questions.

1. What happens in summer?

2. Why is summer beautiful?

Think about the second poem.
Answer the questions.

3. How do you think the people
feel? Tell why.

4. How can you make a day
beautiful?

5. Why do you think the poems
are called "Rainbow Days"?

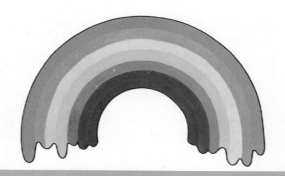

Talk. What makes a day beautiful for you? Listen to your classmate.

WORK WITH A PARTNER

4 Tell Me a Story

Focusing on "After Supper"

Think and Read

▶ Talk. What special person do you like to read with? Tell why.

► Look at the picture on pages 180 and 181. Listen to the poem.

Think about the answers to the questions.

"After Supper"
1. Whom is the poem about?
2. Where are they?
3. What are they doing?
4. What time of day is it?

After Supper

A poem by Dorothy Aldis

Let's not pretend we're anywhere;
Let's only sit here in this chair.

I don't want to play that we
Are sailors sailing on the sea,
Or pirates in a pirates' cave
Or even lions being brave.

I'm feeling very nice and near.
Let's just be here.

Picture by Charles Robinson

Think about the poem.
Answer the questions.

1. What is the boy sharing with the girl?

2. How do you think the boy feels?

3. How do you think the girl feels?

4. The children do not want to pretend. Tell why not.

5. What might the children do next?

Talk. Tell about other things to share after supper. Listen to your classmate.

Focusing on "The Gingerbread Man"

Think and Read

▶ Talk. Tell about something special you have made.

► Listen to the play. Think.
Who ran after the gingerbread
man? Who surprised him?

How would you fill in the
drawing?

Who ran after the
gingerbread man?

Who surprised the
gingerbread man?

The Gingerbread Man

A play adapted from an American folk tale

Pictures by Willi Baum

Characters

Storyteller 1	**Little Old Woman**	**Cow**
Storyteller 2	**Little Old Man**	**Bear**
Storyteller 3	**Gingerbread Man**	**Fox**

Storyteller 1: Once upon a time
a little old woman
and a little old man
lived in a little old house.
They were very happy,
but they had no children.
They wanted a child
of their own.

Storyteller 2: One day the little old woman
was making gingerbread.
She laughed and said,

Little Old Woman: I'll make us a son
out of gingerbread!

Storyteller 3: So she rolled out the dough,
and she cut out a man.
She gave him raisin eyes,
a raisin mouth,
and a coat with raisin buttons.
Then she popped him
into the oven.

Storyteller 1: Before long,
the little old woman looked
to see if the gingerbread man
was done.

Storyteller 2: As soon as the oven door
was opened,
out he jumped!
Off he ran,
out the door,
and down the road.

Little Old Woman: Come back! Come back!

Storyteller 3: Called the little old woman.

Little Old Man: Come back! Come back!

Storyteller 1: Called the little old man.

Storyteller 2: But the gingerbread man
only laughed and said,

Gingerbread Man: Run, run, as fast as you can.
You can't catch me!
I'm the gingerbread man!

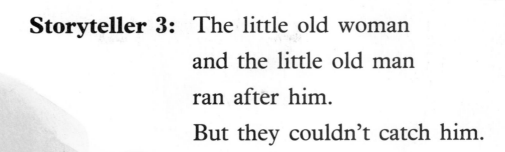

Storyteller 3: The little old woman
and the little old man
ran after him.
But they couldn't catch him.

Storyteller 1: A cow looked up
as the gingerbread man
ran by.
She called,

Cow: Come back! Come back!

Storyteller 2: But the gingerbread man
only laughed and said,

Gingerbread Man: Run, run, as fast as you can.
You can't catch me!
I'm the gingerbread man!
I've run away
From a little old woman,
And a little old man,
And I can run away
From you, too.
I can, I can!

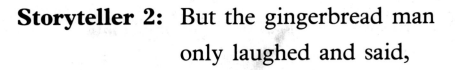

Storyteller 3: The cow ran after
the gingerbread man.
But she couldn't catch him.

Storyteller 1: A bear was looking
for something to eat.
Just then,
the gingerbread man ran by.
The bear called,

Bear: Come back! Come back!

Storyteller 2: But the gingerbread man
only laughed and said,

Gingerbread Man: Run, run, as fast as you can.
You can't catch me!
I'm the gingerbread man!
I've run away
From a little old woman,
And a little old man,
And a cow.
And I can run away
From you, too.
I can, I can!

Storyteller 3: The bear ran after
the gingerbread man.
But he couldn't catch him.

Storyteller 1: Down by the river was a fox.
Along ran the gingerbread man, saying,

Gingerbread Man: Run, run, as fast as you can.
You can't catch me!
I'm the gingerbread man!
I've run away
From a little old woman,
And a little old man,
And a cow,
And a bear.
And I can run away
From you, too.
I can, I can!

Storyteller 2:   But the fox
did not run after him.
She just said sweetly,

Fox: I don't want to catch you,
gingerbread man.
But if you hop on my tail,
I will give you a ride
across the river.

Storyteller 3: The gingerbread man hopped onto the fox's tail. And they started across the river.

Storyteller 1: When the water got deeper, the fox called out,

Fox: Hop on my back
or you will get wet.

Storyteller 2: So the gingerbread man
hopped onto the fox's back.

Storyteller 3: When the water got deeper,
the fox called out,

Fox: Hop on my head
or you will get wet.

Storyteller 1: So the gingerbread man
hopped onto the fox's head.

Storyteller 2: Suddenly
the fox tossed back her head
and opened her mouth.

Storyteller 3: And that was the end
of the gingerbread man
and the end
of this story, too.

Think about the play.
Answer the questions.

1. Why does the little old woman make the gingerbread man?

2. Why does the gingerbread man run away three times?

3. What does the gingerbread man say each time he runs away?

4. How does the fox trick the gingerbread man?

5. What surprises the gingerbread man?

Pretend that the gingerbread man is not tricked by the fox. Talk about how the story would be different.

WORK WITH A PARTNER

In each story, you will see,

There is a mix-up

That you need to fix up.

Which pictures are 1, 2, and 3?

Pictures by Ed Taber

Focusing on "The Little Turtle"

Think and Read

► Talk. What do you know about turtles?

► Listen to the poem. Think.
What does the turtle do?

How would you fill in the
drawing?

What the Turtle Does
1.
2.
3.
4.
5.

The Little Turtle

A poem by Vachel Lindsay

Pictures by Larry Mikec

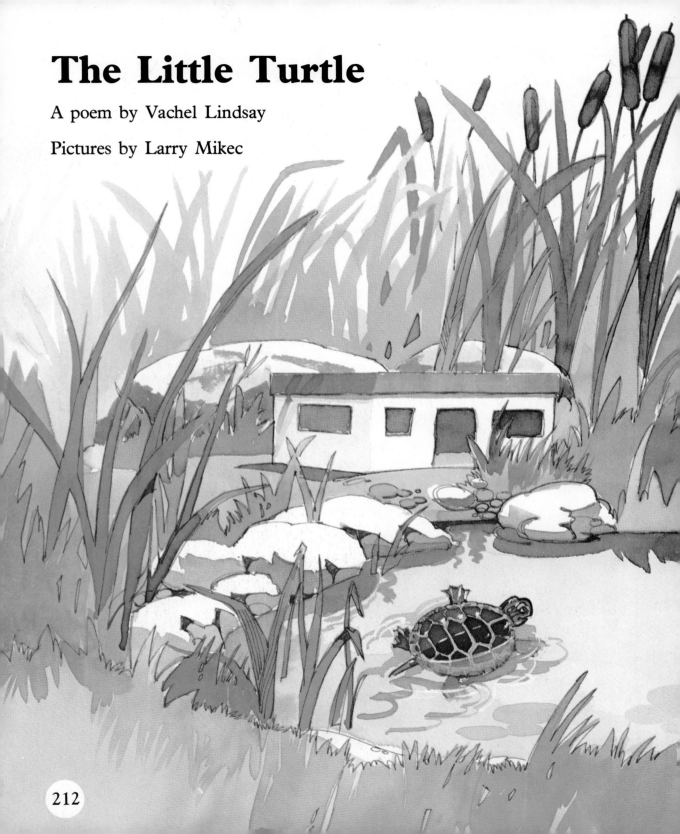

There was a little turtle.

He lived in a box.

He swam in a puddle.

He climbed on the rocks.

He snapped at a mosquito.
He snapped at a flea.
He snapped at a minnow.
And he snapped at me.

He caught the mosquito.
He caught the flea.
He caught the minnow.
But he didn't catch me.

Think about the poem.
Answer the questions.

1. Where does the turtle live?

2. How does the turtle move from place to place?

3. What does the turtle eat?

4. Why does the girl watch the turtle?

5. What might the turtle do next?

Talk. Tell what a turtle needs to live. Ask questions.

Think and Read

▶ Talk. What do you know about goats?

▶ Listen to the story.
Think. What does each Billy
Goat do at the bridge?

How would you fill in this
drawing?

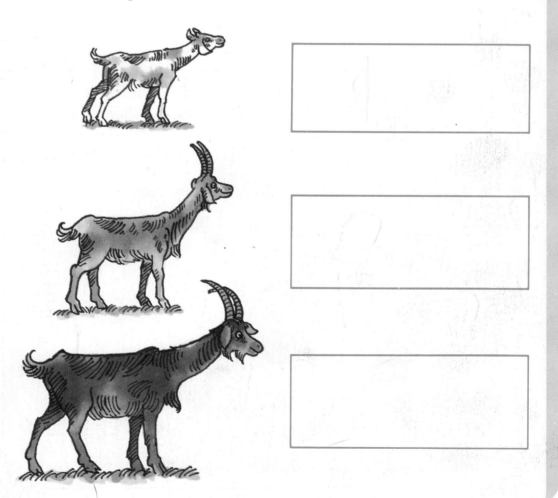

The Three Billy Goats Gruff

A Norwegian folk tale collected by P. C. Asbjörnsen
and Jörgen E. Moe

Pictures by Willi Baum

Once on a time there were
three Billy Goats who were to go up
to the hillside to make themselves fat.
And the name of all three
was "Gruff."

On the way up was a bridge
over a river they had to cross.
And under the bridge
lived a great ugly Troll,
with eyes as big as saucers
and a nose as long as a poker.

221

So first of all came
the youngest Billy Goat Gruff
to cross the bridge.

"*Trip, trap! Trip, trap!*"
went the bridge.

"*Who's that* tripping
over my bridge?" roared the Troll.

"Oh! It is only I, the tiniest
Billy Goat Gruff. I'm going up
to the hillside to make myself fat,"
said the Billy Goat, with such a
small voice.

"Now, I'm going to gobble you up,"
said the Troll.

"Oh, no! Please don't take me.
I'm too little," said the Billy Goat.
"Wait a bit 'til
the second Billy Goat Gruff comes.
He's much bigger."

"Well! Be off with you,"
said the Troll.

A little while after
the second Billy Goat Gruff
came to cross the bridge.

"TRIP, TRAP! TRIP, TRAP!
TRIP, TRAP!" went the bridge.

"WHO'S THAT tripping
over my bridge?" roared the Troll.

"Oh! It's the second
Billy Goat Gruff.
I'm going up to the hillside
to make myself fat," said the Billy Goat,
with a voice that was not so small.

"Now, I'm going to gobble you up,"
said the Troll.

"Oh, no! Don't take me.
Wait a little 'til
the big Billy Goat Gruff comes.
He's much bigger."

"Very well! Be off with you,"
said the Troll.

225

Just then up came
the big Billy Goat Gruff.

"TRIP, TRAP! TRIP, TRAP!
TRIP, TRAP! TRIP, TRAP!"
went the bridge.

"WHO'S THAT tramping
over my bridge?" roared the Troll.

"IT'S I!
THE BIG BILLY GOAT GRUFF,"
said the Billy Goat, who had a big, ugly
voice of his own.

"Now, I'm going
to gobble you up,"
roared the Troll.

"Well, come along!"
said the big Billy Goat Gruff.
"I've got two big spears
to fight you with."

So he flew at the Troll
and tossed him out into the river.

227

Then he went up to the hillside.
There the three Billy Goats
got so fat that they were not able
to walk home again.

And if the fat hasn't fallen off them,
why they're still fat.

And so—

"Snip, snap, snout,
This tale's told out."

Think about the story.
Answer the questions.

1. What happens when the first two Billy Goats get to the bridge?

2. What happens when the big Billy Goat gets to the bridge?

3. Were you surprised by the story ending? Tell why or why not.

4. What does the Troll learn?

5. How would the story be different if the Troll were kind?

Talk. Which Billy Goat do you think is the smartest?
Tell why.

**WORK IN
A GROUP**

Learn About
STORIES

One, Two, Three—Surprise!

Some stories tell about things
that happen one, two, three times.
Then there is a surprise ending!

Here is a story you know.
Draw or tell the end of the story.

The Three Billy Goats Gruff

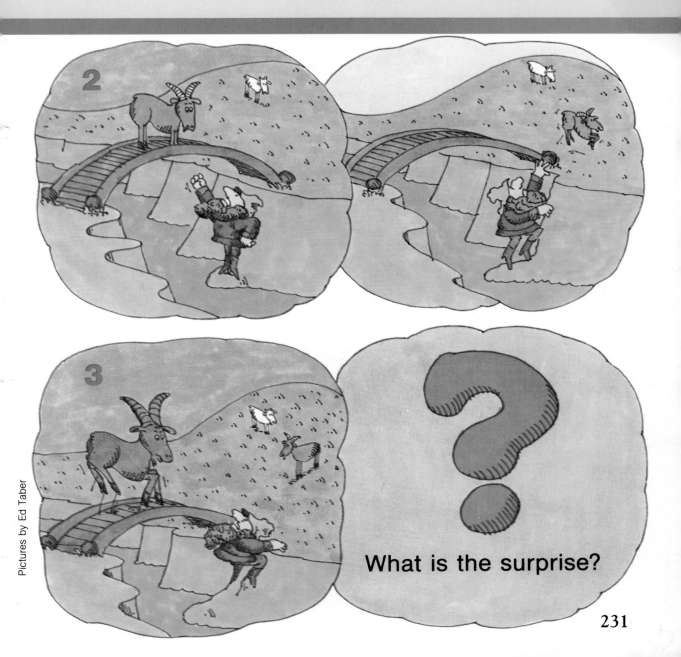

What is the surprise?

231

Now tell your own story.

Maggie reached into her magic hat one, two, three times.

Tell or draw what happens the last time.

Make your ending a surprise.

Maggie's Magic Hat

What is the surprise?

Focusing on "What Animals Need"

Think and Read

▶ Talk. What do people need to live?

► Listen to the information story.
Think. Name each animal.
How does each animal get what
it needs?

How would you fill in the chart?

Animal	What It Needs

What Animals Need

People and animals are alike in some ways.

They both need to eat food and drink water to live and grow.

This animal is a deer.

The deer is thirsty.

What does the deer drink?

Different animals eat different foods.
This animal is a grasshopper.
A grasshopper is an insect.
What is the grasshopper eating?

This fish is an animal.

It lives in a stream.

The fish is hungry.

It finds an insect to eat.

Insects are food for the fish.

This animal is a bear.

It goes to a stream and looks for a fish to catch.

The bear will eat the fish for food.

What do you eat when you are hungry?

What do you drink when you are thirsty?

Think about the information story.
Answer the questions.

1. What do all animals need to live?

2. How does a bear get what it needs?

3. Why is the stream important to the deer?

4. What is different about what the grasshopper and the bear eat?

5. How do people get what they need to live?

Talk. What other animals do you
know about? What do they eat?
What do they drink?

5 Far, Far Away

Focusing on "Where Go the Boats?"

Think and Read

► Talk. What do you know about boats?

► Listen to the poem. Think.
What do the boats pass?

How would you fill in the
drawing?

What
do the
boats pass?

1.
2.
3.

245

Where Go the Boats?

A poem by Robert Louis Stevenson

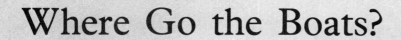

Dark brown is the river,
Golden is the sand.
It flows along forever,
With trees on either hand.

Green leaves a-floating,
Castles of the foam,
Boats of mine a-boating—
Where will all come home?

246

On goes the river,
And out past the mill,
Away down the valley,
Away down the hill.

Away down the river,
A hundred miles or more,
Other little children
Shall bring my boats ashore.

Picture by Christa Kieffer

247

Think about the poem.
Answer the questions.

1. Where are the boats going?

2. What do the boats pass?

3. What happens to the boats down the river?

4. Why are the children sailing the boats?

5. How do you think the children feel?

Talk. Why do you think people like to sail toy boats?

WORK WITH A PARTNER

Focusing on "Sebastian and the Bee"

▶ Talk. What do you know about bees?

▶ Read the picture story. Think. What happens to Sebastian?

How would you fill in the drawing?

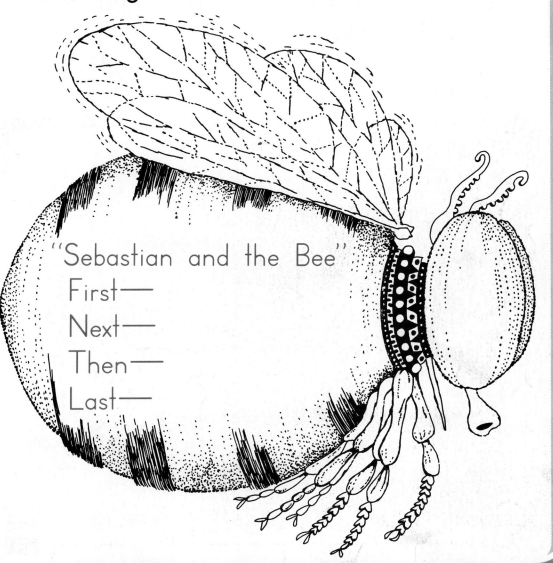

"Sebastian and the Bee"
First—
Next—
Then—
Last—

Sebastian

A picture story by Fernando Krahn

and the Bee

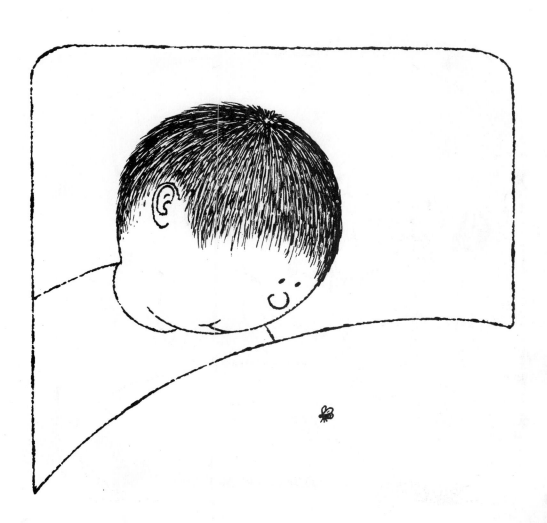

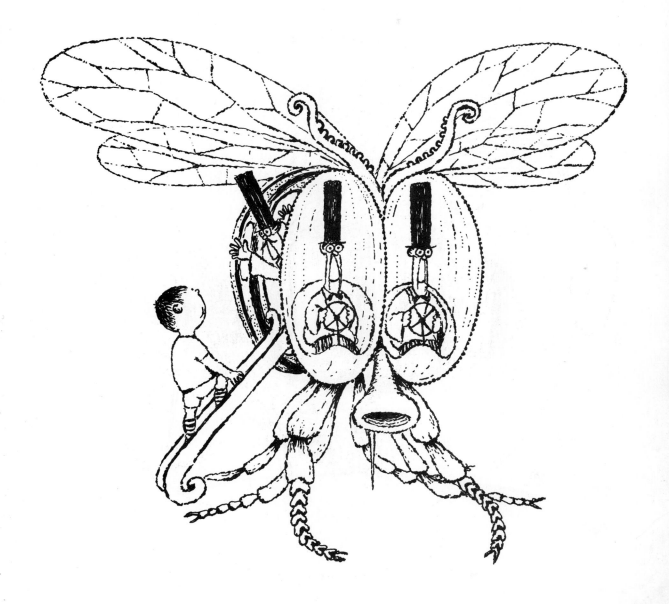

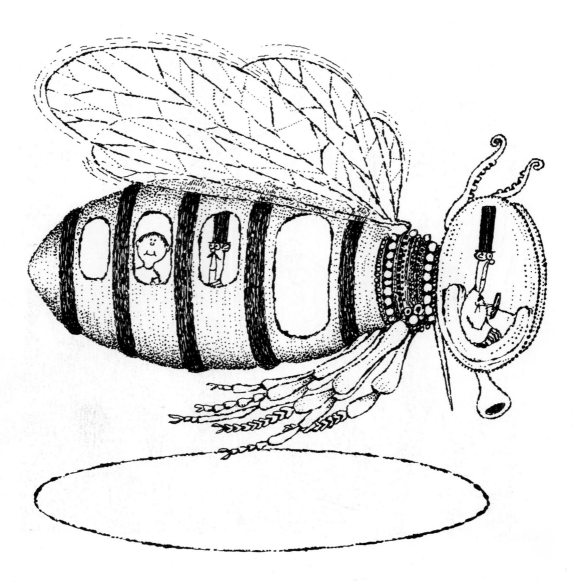

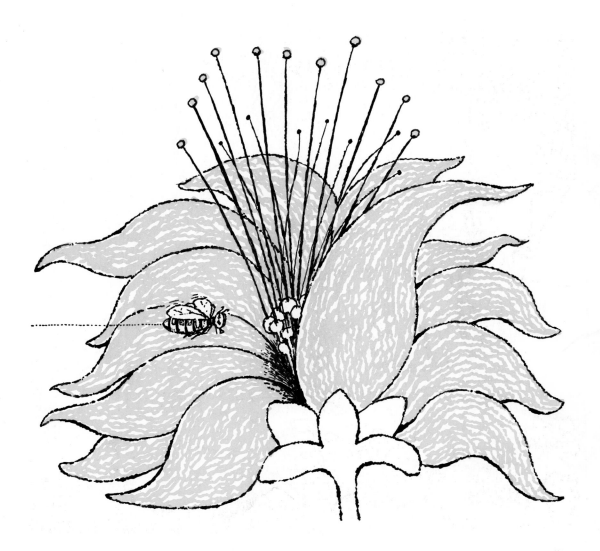

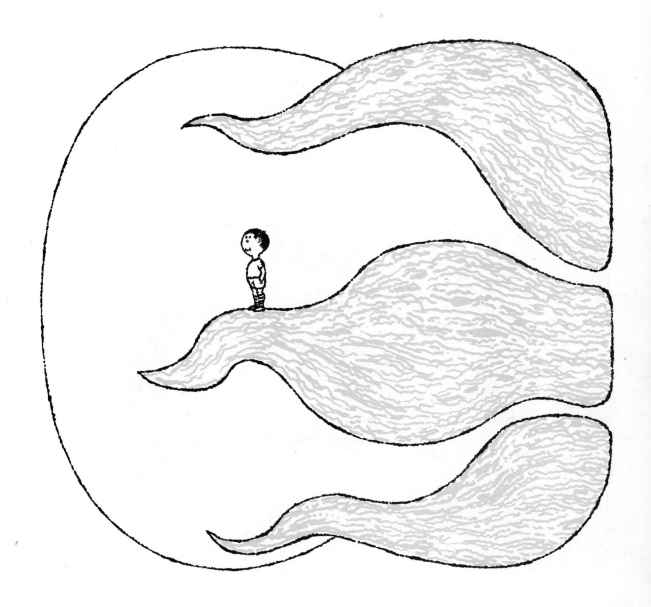

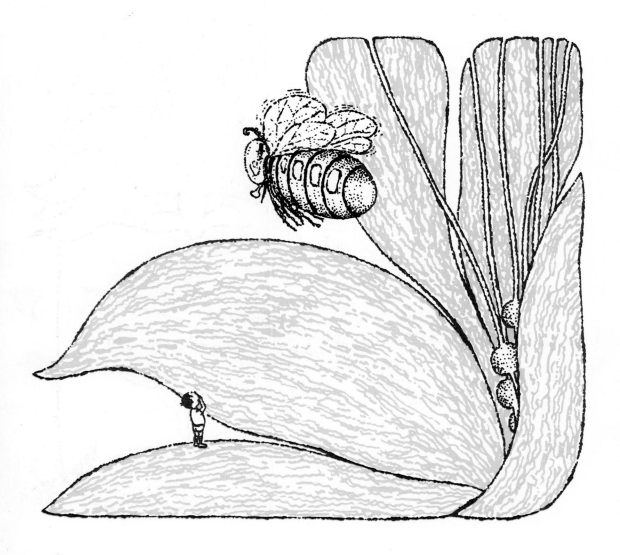

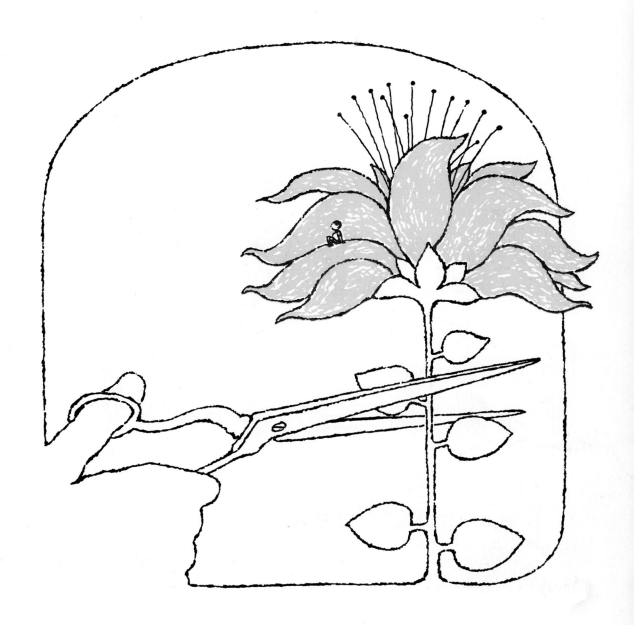

About
FERNANDO KRAHN

(To be read by the teacher)

Do you like to draw pictures? Here is someone who has been drawing pictures since he was a child. He is Fernando Krahn, who drew the story <u>Sebastian and the Bee</u>.

Mr. Krahn, who was born in Chile, a country in South America, has said, "I can tell a story just through drawings, and that satisfies me greatly." Most of Mr. Krahn's books, which include several stories about the adventures of Sebastian, have no words. They are told through pictures alone.

More Books by Fernando Krahn

The Self-Made Snowman
The Journeys of Sebastian
Sebastian and the Mushroom
The Mystery of the Giant's Footprints
The Secret in the Dungeon

270

Think about the picture story.
Answer the questions.

1. Is Sebastian's trip a real one or a dream?

2. What does Sebastian do before he rides inside the bee?

3. How does Sebastian feel before the trip?

4. How does he feel after the trip?

5. Which part of the story do you like the best?

Talk. Pretend you are very small. What would you ride in? Where would you go?

WORK WITH A PARTNER

Learn About
THE LIBRARY

Rabbit Gets a Library Book

Pictures by Ed Taber

Think and Read

▶ Talk. How do people take care of a pet dog?

► Listen to the story.
Think about what Harry does.
How would you answer these
questions?

What happens first?

What happens next?

What happens last?

HARRY
The Dirty Dog

A story by Gene Zion

Pictures by Margaret Bloy Graham

Harry was a white dog with <u>black</u>
spots who liked everything,
except . . . getting a bath.
So one day when he heard the water
running in the tub,
he took the scrubbing brush . . .

and buried it in the back yard.

Then he ran away from home.

He played where they were fixing the street

and got very dirty.

He played at the railroad

and got even dirtier.

He played tag with other dogs

and became dirtier still.

He slid down a coal chute
and got the dirtiest of all.
In fact, he changed

from a white dog with black spots
to a black dog with white spots.

Although there were many other things to do,
Harry began to wonder if his family thought
that he had really run away.

He felt tired and hungry too,
so without stopping on the way
he ran back home.

When Harry got to his house,
he crawled through the fence
and sat looking at the back door.

One of the family looked out and said,
"There's a strange dog in the back yard . . .
by the way, has anyone seen Harry?"

When Harry heard this, he tried very hard
to show them he was Harry. He started to do
all his old, clever tricks. He flip-flopped

and he flop-flipped.
He rolled over and played dead.

He danced and he sang.

He did these tricks over and over again,
but everyone shook his head and said,
Oh, no, it couldn't be Harry."

Harry gave up
and walked slowly toward the gate,
but suddenly he stopped.

He ran to a corner of the garden
and started to dig furiously.
Soon he jumped away from the hole,
barking short, happy barks.

He'd found the scrubbing brush!
And carrying it in his mouth,
he ran into the house.

Up the stairs he dashed,
with the family
following close behind.

He jumped into the bathtub and sat up begging,
with the scrubbing brush in his mouth,
a trick he certainly had never done before.

"This little doggie wants a bath!"
cried the little girl, and her father said,
"Why don't you and your brother give him one?"

Harry's bath was the soapiest one he'd ever had.
It worked like magic. As soon as the children
started to scrub, they began shouting,
"Mummy! Daddy! Look, look! Come quick!"

"It's Harry! It's Harry! It's Harry!" they cried.
Harry wagged his tail and was very, very happy.
His family combed and brushed him lovingly, and
he became once again a white dog with black spots.

It was wonderful to be home.
After dinner, Harry fell asleep
in his favorite place, happily dreaming
of how much fun it had been getting dirty.
He slept so soundly,
he didn't even feel the scrubbing brush
he'd hidden under his pillow.

Think about the story.
Answer the questions.

1. Why does Harry hide the scrubbing brush?

2. How does Harry get so dirty?

3. Why does Harry go home?

4. Why does Harry want to have a bath?

5. What do you think Harry learned?

Pretend Harry is dirty again.
Talk about how Harry feels.
Tell what Harry does.

WORK IN
A GROUP

Focusing on "Pets and People"

Think and Read

▶ Talk. What kinds of animals do people keep as pets?

▶ Listen to the information story. Think. How do people take care of pets?

How would you finish the drawing?

Ways People Care for Pets

1.
2.
3.
4.
5.

Connections

Pets and People

There are many kinds of pets.

Dogs and cats can be pets.

Birds and hamsters can be pets.

What other animals can be pets?

Look at the children in the picture.

What pets do they have?

Children play with their pets.

They must also take care of them.

How are these boys and girls taking care of their pets?

Some pets need special homes.

Their homes must be kept clean.

Where do pet birds live?

Where do pet fish live?

How can children keep their pets'
homes clean?

Pets sometimes get sick, just as people do.

Veterinarians help sick pets get well.

How is this veterinarian helping a pet dog?

Think about the information story. Answer the questions.

1. In what ways are pets alike?

2. In what ways are pets different?

3. How can people help pets?

4. How is caring for a dog the same as caring for a cat?

5. Which other animals would be good pets? Tell why.

Talk. Why is it important to take care of pets?

Focusing on "The Horses"

▶ Talk. What do you know about horses?

▶ Listen to the poem. Think.
What do horses look like?

How would you fill in the
drawing?

Words That Tell About Horses

1.   3.

2.   4.

The Horses

A poem by Elizabeth Coatsworth

Red horse,
Roan horse,
Black horse,
And white,
Feeding all together in the green
    summer light.

White horse,
Black horse,
Spotted horse,
And gray,
I wish that I were off with you,
    far, far away!

Picture by Kazuhiko Sano

Think about the poem.
Answer the questions.

1. Who is talking to the horses?

2. What is the boy's wish?

3. How do you think the boy feels about horses? Tell why.

4. How are the horses different?

5. How are the horses alike?

Talk. Where would you go if you could be far, far away?

6 I'm Growing

Focusing on "Okay Everybody!"

Think and Read ▶ Talk. What can you do now that you could not do when you were smaller?

▶ **Listen to the poem. Think.
What things are taller than the
boy?**

**How would you fill in the
drawing?**

Things That Are Taller Than the Boy
1.
2.
3.
4.
5.

Okay Everybody!

A poem by Karla Kuskin

Okay everybody, listen to this:

I am tired of being smaller

Than you

And them

And him

And trees and buildings.

So watch out

All you gorillas and adults

Beginning tomorrow morning

Boy

Am I going to be taller.

Picture by Raphael & Bolognese

Think about the poem.
Answer the questions.

1. About whom is the poem?

2. What is the boy's wish?

3. Why does the boy wish to be taller?

4. Why might gorillas and adults seem the same to the boy?

5. How do you think the boy will feel tomorrow? Tell why.

Talk. What could you do if you were taller?

Focusing on "The New Baby Calf"

Think and Read

▶ Talk. How does a mother animal take care of her babies?

▶ Listen to the poem. Think.
What does the new baby calf
like?

How would you finish this list?

Things the New Baby Calf Likes

1.

2.

3.

4.

5.

The New Baby Calf

A poem by Edith H. Newlin

Buttercup, the cow, had a new baby calf,
a fine baby calf,
a strong baby calf,
Not strong like his mother
But strong for a calf,
For *this* baby calf was so *new!*

Buttercup licked him with her strong warm
   tongue,
Buttercup washed him with her strong warm
   tongue,
Buttercup brushed him with her strong warm
   tongue,
   And the new baby calf *liked that*!

The new baby calf took a very little walk,
a tiny little walk,
a teeny little walk,
But his long legs wobbled
When he took a little walk,
And the new baby calf fell down.

Buttercup told him with a low soft "Moo-oo!"
That he was doing very well for one so very new
And she talked very gently, as mother cows do,
And the new baby calf *liked that*!

The new baby calf took another little walk,
a little longer walk,
a little stronger walk,
He walked around his mother and he found
the place to drink.
And the new baby calf liked *that*!

Buttercup told him with another low moo
That drinking milk from mother was a fine thing
    to do,
That she had lots of milk for him and for the
    farmer, too,
And the new baby calf liked *that*!

The new baby calf drank milk every day,
His legs grew so strong that he could run and
    play,
He learned to eat grass and then grain and hay,
    And the big baby calf grew fat!

Think about the story.
Answer the questions.

1. What happens when the calf takes his first walk?

2. What does Buttercup tell her calf when he falls down?

3. How do you think the calf feels about Buttercup?

4. How does the new baby calf change?

5. How are Buttercup and the new baby calf different?

Talk. What new things have you learned to do this year?

WORK IN A GROUP

Focusing on "Penguins"

Think and Read

▶ Talk. What do you know about penguins?

► Listen to the information story. Think.
How does a baby penguin
change?

How would you answer the
question?

How does a baby
penguin change?

1.
2.
3.
4.

Penguins

When spring comes, the penguins
make a nest.
They pile up little rocks.

Pictures by Tom Dunnington

The penguins' nest is ready!
Mother penguin lays an egg.
She keeps it warm.
Father penguin helps.

The egg cracks!
Out comes the baby penguin.
The baby needs food.
Mother goes to catch fish.
Father keeps the baby warm.

Mother comes back with food.

She feeds the baby.

Now it is Father's turn.

Mother will keep the baby warm.

Father will catch fish.

The baby penguins are growing!

They are almost as big as their mothers and fathers.

Now they can stay alone.

Their mothers and fathers go fishing.

The babies crowd together to keep warm.

Penguins have wings, but they do not fly.

They walk on the ice.

Wings keep the penguins from falling or slipping.

Look at the picture.

How do penguins use their wings in the water?

Now the baby penguins are grown.
They do not look like babies.
How have they changed?

Someday they will make nests.
There will be more baby penguins!

Think about the information story.
Answer the questions.

1. How is a baby penguin different from its mother and father?

2. What does a baby penguin need?

3. What must a baby penguin learn?

4. Why are a baby penguin's parents busy?

5. How are penguins different from other birds?

Talk. How have you changed since you were a baby?

WORK IN A GROUP

349

Focusing on "He Bear, She Bear"

Think and Read

▶ Talk. What jobs do you do in the classroom?

▶ Listen to the story. Think. What is the main idea of the story?

How would you answer the question?

What is the main idea?

He Bear, She Bear

He Bear, She Bear

Adapted from the story in verse by Stan and Jan Berenstain

Pictures by Tony Kenyon

There are many things to be.
Come on, He Bear, follow me!

We could fix a clock,
Paint a door,
Build a house,
Have a store.

We could be doctors
And make people well.
We could teach kids
How to add and spell.

353

I may build bridges,
I may climb poles,
I may race cars,
I may dig holes.

I could be a magician,
I could go on TV.
I could study the fish
Who live in the sea.

We'll jump and dig and build and fly. . .
There is *nothing* that we cannot try.
We can do all these things, you see,
Whether we are he OR she.

Think about the story.
Answer the questions.

1. What do He Bear and She Bear tell each other?

2. What jobs could He Bear and She Bear do?

3. Who might teach He Bear and She Bear to do the jobs?

4. How do He Bear and She Bear feel at the end of the story?

5. Which job would you want? Tell why.

Talk about workers in your school. What jobs do they do?

WORK IN A GROUP

Some words in stories tell how things sound.

When the Wind blows,
the sound is
"you-ou-ou."

When the Gunniwolf runs,
the sound is
"hunker-cha, hunker-cha."

When the Billy Goats Gruff walk
over the bridge,
the sound is
"trip, trap, trip, trap."

Pictures by Ed Taber

Get ready to read a story about us.

These things are in the story.

Make up words to tell how each thing sounds.

Say your sounds for these things
as you read the story
on the next page.

The Hare and the Tortoise

The hare and the tortoise
had a race.

The hare started.

The tortoise started, too.

The hare swam across a lake.

The tortoise swam across the lake, too.

The hare went
through a pile of leaves.

The tortoise went
through the pile of leaves, too.

The hare took a nap.

The tortoise kept going.

The hare woke up and ran.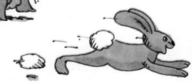

But the tortoise won the race!

Think and Read

▶ Talk. When do you get special presents?

▶ Listen to the story. Think.
What is the main idea of each
part of the story?

How would you fill in
the drawings?

"Peach"

"Summer"

"Rain"

UMBRELLA

Adapted from the story by Taro Yashima

Pictures by Taro Yashima

Momo (Peach)

Momo is the name of a little girl
who was born in New York.
The word *Momo* means
"the peach" in Japan
where her father and mother
used to live.

On her third birthday
Momo was given two presents—
red rubber boots and an umbrella!
They pleased her so much
that she even woke up that night
to take another look at them.

Natsu (Summer)

But it was still summer,
and the sun was bright.

Every morning
Momo asked her mother,
"Why doesn't the rain fall?"
The answer was always the same,
"Wait, wait. It will come."

***Ame* (Rain)**

It was many, many days later
that finally the rain fell.
Momo was wakened
by her mother calling,
"Get up! Get up!
What a surprise for you!"

371

Momo did not stop to wash her face.
She even pulled the boots
onto her bare feet—
she was so excited.

The sidewalk was all wet and new.
Raindrops were jumping all over,
like tiny people dancing.

The street was crowded and noisy.
But she said to herself,
"I must walk straight,
like a grown-up."

375

On the umbrella,
raindrops made a wonderful music
she never had heard before—
     Bon polo
     bon polo
     ponpolo ponpolo
     ponpolo ponpolo
     bolo bolo ponpolo
     bolo bolo ponpolo
     boto boto ponpolo
     boto boto ponpolo

The rain did not stop all day long.
Momo watched it at times
while she was playing the games
at the nursery school.

She did not forget her umbrella
when her father came
to take her home.
She used to forget
other things so easily—
but not her umbrella.

381

The street was crowded and noisy.
But she said to herself,
"I must walk straight,
like a grown-up!"

On her umbrella,
the raindrops made the wonderful music—

Bon polo

bon polo

ponpolo ponpolo

ponpolo ponpolo

bolo bolo ponpolo

bolo bolo ponpolo

boto boto ponpolo

boto boto ponpolo

all the way home.

About
TARO YASHIMA

(**To be read by the teacher**)

As soon as Taro Yashima gets an idea for a story, he writes it on a piece of paper. Then he puts the paper in an envelope until he is ready to write the story.

Many of his stories began because his daughter, Momo, wanted to know what he did as a boy in Japan. A few of Taro Yashima's stories are about Momo. He wrote one of his favorite stories, Umbrella, as a gift for Momo's eighth birthday.

More Books by Taro Yashima
Crow Boy
Seashore Story
Momo's Kitten
Village Tree
Youngest One

Think about the story.
Answer the questions.

1. What presents are given to Momo?

2. How does Momo feel about the presents?

3. Why does Momo have to wait to use the presents?

4. How does Momo show she is growing up?

5. Pretend that you are Momo. How would you thank your mother and father for the presents?

Talk about a time when you gave someone a present.

WORK IN A GROUP

387

WORD SPOT
Words, Pictures, Meanings

Aa Bb

Aa

animals   We see many <u>animals</u> at the zoo.

Bb

beak   The bird picks up a bug with its <u>beak</u>.

beautiful   A rose is a <u>beautiful</u> flower.

bee   The <u>bee</u> flew around the flowers.

black   My doll has <u>black</u> hair.

boots   Those <u>boots</u> will keep your feet warm.

bridge   We drive over a <u>bridge</u> to cross the river.

brown   The football is <u>brown</u>.

brushed   I <u>brushed</u> my long hair.

buried   The dog <u>buried</u> a bone in the ground.

Cc

called   Mother <u>called</u> for Sam to come inside.

carries   The wind <u>carries</u> the kite into the air.

Cc   Dd

chameleon We saw the <u>chameleon</u> change its color.

chews Kim <u>chews</u> her food well when she eats.

colors The <u>colors</u> of the painting are bright.

cracks She <u>cracks</u> the egg before she cooks it.

crawled The baby <u>crawled</u> on the floor.

Dd

danced We <u>danced</u> to the music.

deer The <u>deer</u> drinks water at the river.

doctors   <u>Doctors</u> take care of sick people.

dough   We mix <u>dough</u> to make bread.

Ee

earth   The farmer plants seeds in the <u>earth</u>.

elephant   The <u>elephant</u> sprays water with its long nose.

Ff

fall   In <u>fall</u> the weather gets cooler.

farmyard   Pigs run around the <u>farmyard</u>.

Ff

feathers   The duck's <u>feathers</u> are soft and white.

feeds   The mother bird <u>feeds</u> her babies worms.

fine   My mother said I did a <u>fine</u> job.

flea   The tiny <u>flea</u> bit the dog.

floats   A sailboat <u>floats</u> in water.

flour   Use <u>flour</u> to make bread.

frog   A <u>frog</u> eats bugs for dinner.

Gg

golden   The leaves on the ground are golden, not green.

gorillas   The gorillas are the biggest apes at the zoo.

grabs   The boy grabs the kite string.

grasshopper   The green grasshopper jumps high.

gray   The shirt has gray stripes.

green   The green leaves turn red in the fall.

Hh

Hh

hamsters Some hamsters look like mice.

helps The mother cat helps her kittens find food.

hen The hen lives in the barn.

hippos When it is hot, hippos stay in the water.

horns The goat has two sharp horns on its head.

hungry My hungry dog ate all its food.

Jj

jumped   The frog <u>jumped</u> into the pond.

Ll

laughed   Bob <u>laughed</u> when he saw the funny clown.

lays   The chicken <u>lays</u> eggs in the nest.

leopard   A big cat with spots is called a <u>leopard</u>.

loaf   Mother made a <u>loaf</u> of bread.

Mm Nn Oo

Mm

mill　Wheat is ground into flour at the <u>mill</u>.

minnow　A <u>minnow</u> swims with the larger fish.

mosquito　A <u>mosquito</u> flew into the house.

Nn

neither　I have <u>neither</u> a pencil nor a book.

new　Amy bought a <u>new</u> watch.

Oo

opened　Bill <u>opened</u> many boxes.

ostrich   An <u>ostrich</u> runs fast but does not fly.

─────────────

─────────────

penguin   A <u>penguin</u> is a large black and white bird.

pirates   Those <u>pirates</u> are looking for gold.

poles   <u>Poles</u> hold up telephone wires.

prairie dogs   <u>Prairie dogs</u> live in tunnels under the ground.

Pp Rr Ss

pretend Henry likes to pretend he is a pirate.

puddle The bird splashes in the puddle of water.

Rr

ripe Some apples are red when they are ripe.

river We sail boats in the river.

Ss

sandwich Dad made a sandwich for lunch.

sang   We <u>sang</u> funny songs.

saucer   Milk spilled from the cup into the
               <u>saucer</u>.

season   In some places, winter is a cold
               <u>season</u>.

shoulders The boy sat on his father's <u>shoulders</u>.

slid   The penguin <u>slid</u> down the icy hill.

snail   That <u>snail</u> is not hiding in its shell.

soft   The kitten's fur is very <u>soft</u>.

special   My grandmother is a <u>special</u> person.

Ss   Tt

spinning The top is <u>spinning</u> very fast.

spring New leaves grow on trees in <u>spring</u>.

strong A <u>strong</u> child can lift the box.

summer This <u>summer</u> we will swim in the lake.

Tt

tall The giraffe is a very <u>tall</u> animal.

thirsty I drink water when I am <u>thirsty</u>.

tiger Look at the stripes on the <u>tiger</u>.

toaster Use a <u>toaster</u> to toast bread.

tooth A new <u>tooth</u> grew where the old one fell out.

tossed We <u>tossed</u> the ball to each other.

troll The story is about a little <u>troll</u>.

turtle The little green <u>turtle</u> has a hard shell.

tusks The elephant's <u>tusks</u> are long and white.

twice My dad is <u>twice</u> as big as I am.

Uu

umbrella I use an <u>umbrella</u> when it rains.

Ww   Zz

Ww

wagged   The dog <u>wagged</u> its long tail.

white   The fresh snow is <u>white</u> and clean.

winter   Last <u>winter</u> was very cold.

wonder   I <u>wonder</u> why the sun shines.

Zz

zebra   A <u>zebra</u> has black and white stripes.